SEEKING PEACE
THROUGH RECONCILIATION

MANAGING ANGER, CONFLICTS, AND
DIFFERENCES IN RELATIONSHIPS

A WORKBOOK COMPANION
FOR PERSONAL STUDY

DONALD E. JONES, PHD

J & A BOOK PUBLISHERS
www.jabookpublishers.com

ISBN-10:1-946368-08-3
ISBN-13:978-1-946368-08-9

DEDICATION

I dedicate this book to my Savior and Lord Jesus Christ. He has been with me every step of my journey upon the Earth, and I so look forward to being in His presence forever and ever.

CONTENTS

ACKNOWLEDGMENTS

I want to thank my wonderful and gracious wife Carol who has supported me in this ministry with sacrifice, enthusiasm, encouragement, and accountability. Most of all, she has been a constant blessing because of her willingness to listen. I was always sharing with her the truths God had been teaching me as I studied His word and wrote this book. It consumed many hours. Thank you, Carol, and I deeply love you.

I want to thank my son Gregory R. Jones for volunteering to be the primary editor of this important book. Without his time and effort in painstakingly and meticulously going over every word and every sentence checking and rechecking the sentence structure and grammar, I would not have been able to complete it. Thank you for your ministry to me. I love you my son.

I want to thank my other children, Krista, Matt, and Kara for their love for Christ and His Word and their willingness to live for Him. I love you all.

Introduction

This workbook is designed to aid in the comprehension and application of the truths from the Scriptures which are found in the book of the same name. It has a question and answer format because asking questions was a powerful teaching method that the Lord used to reveal God's divine truth. Jesus asked over one hundred and thirty questions as He instructed the people of God and others. These are only the recorded ones. We can only speculate as to how many questions He might have actually asked. The Lord used His questioning techniques to prompt His listeners to focus, understand, analyze, evaluate, and apply the principles He was proclaiming to them. The same has been done in this workbook.

In Matthew 12, Mark 3, and Luke 6, the three of the four gospel writers describe the healing of a man's withered hand in a synagogue. As a recognized Rabbi, Jesus would attend a synagogue service and be allowed to speak. Here He would preach the kingdom of God. On one such occasion, a group of Pharisees were in attendance and noticed a man in the synagogue with a withered hand. This would be a perfect opportunity to accuse Jesus of breaking their laws if they could get Him to heal the crippled man on this Sabbath day. To force the issue, they posed a question. In Matthew 12:10, the apostle writes, "And behold there was a man with a withered hand. They asked him, 'Is it lawful to heal on the Sabbath day?' that they might accuse him."

The Jewish scholars had added many additional customs, rules and regulations to God's law over the years which had taken on the same importance as the God's Word. Yet, these were man-made burdens they placed on the people. One of these was the custom that no work of any kind should be done on the Sabbath. To the Pharisees this meant almost any kind of labor, deeds, or works including a miracle.

The Lord knew this foolish rule and also knew that God's law indicated that no labor for profit was to be done in order for His people to have a time of rest. This in no way was to inhibit His people from good works toward others. When Jesus saw the crippled man, He felt compassion for Him and desired to make him whole again. The Lord also knew what was in the Pharisees' evil hearts as they yearned for this supposed violation. To challenge them, Jesus commanded the man to stand up and position himself in the middle of the synagogue. He wanted all to see what He was about to do.

Then, Jesus turned to these self-righteous hypocrites and rather than answering their question, posed two of His own and answered them Himself. In Luke 6:9, Luke records, "Then Jesus said to them, 'I will ask you something: Is it lawful on the Sabbath to do good, or to do harm? To save a life, or to kill?'" Immediately after this in Matthew 12:11-12 it says, "He said to them, 'What man is there among you, who has one sheep, and if this one falls into a pit on the Sabbath day, won't he grab on to it, and lift it out? Of how much more value then is a man than a sheep! Therefore it is lawful to do good on the Sabbath day.'" Jesus rebuked the Pharisees with a two stinging questions and a chastising answer. No man would allow his sheep to die on the Sabbath, and the crippled man was worth much more.

He commanded the man to stretch out his hand toward the Lord and healed him! The Pharisees were speechless. They had been bested by the Lord with two penetrating questions. As Jesus used questions, so shall we. May these important questions help you focus, understand, analyze, evaluate, and apply these important biblical principles.

2

Chapter 1

Put Anger Away

The biggest hindrance in the reconciliation process will come from our anger. This raging emotion can rear its ugly head during every step in the restoration of a relationship and must be dealt with.

In the section, "A Typical Scenario," the author describes an angry exchange between two brothers over a family reunion which will require a reconciliation.

What is the scenario about?

What did the conflict concern?

What was the relationship between the parties?

Have you had a similar experience?

In the section, "A Scriptural Principle" the author presents an important biblical principle in the process of reconciliation which concerns eliminating our anger.

How would you express this principle in your own words?

How would you rewrite this principle to make it even more personal to your life (using your name and situation)?

Why do you think this principle might be important in your life right now?

How would you rate yourself on the percentage of times you followed this principle in the past when you did something wrong in a relationship?

Directions: Put a horizontal mark and your name where you see yourself on the percentage line.

| 0% | 25% | 50% | 75% | 100% |

In the section, "A Biblical Explanation," the author explains the reasons why we must eliminate our anger whenever it arises and how to do it.

According to Ephesians 4:31 and Colossians 3:8, what are Christians supposed to do with their anger?

According to Psalm 37:8, what is the eventual result of all expressions of anger?

According to Ephesians 4:26, are angry feelings sinful? Why or why not?

According to Psalm 4:4, what is the first step in the process of eliminating anger?

What are the second and third steps in removing anger?

In what ways might these truths impact your relationships?

In the section, "An Ancient Portrait," the author provides a unique portrayal of the relationship between Saul and David and how it went awry.

What had David done to make Saul have such affection for him?

What suddenly caused Saul to become so angry at David?

What did Saul do with his anger that caused it to become even more intense?

How did Saul involve his two daughters and son in his evil schemes to kill David?

What were some of David righteous responses as he was running from Saul?

Have you ever been in any situation comparable to Saul's jealousy or David's innocence? How was it different? How was it the same?

In the section, "A Modern Anecdote," the author discusses a situation involving a widowed senior, his neighbor, and a barking dog which needed reconciliation.

Why was the widowed senior so angry with his neighbor?

What were some of the ways the widowed senior attempted to cope with the barking dog?

Rather than confront the neighbor, what did the senior do?

What finally happened that made him come to his senses?

How should God's Word be involved in this situation?

Based on the truths learned in this chapter, what would you do if you were the widowed senior annoyed by the barking dog or the neighbor unaffected by the barking dog?

In the section, "A Personal Response," the author provides a model you may use for prayer if you find it necessary after discovering the truths in this chapter.

Are you presently in a relationship where you have sinned against another and have not asked God for forgiveness? If not, is there one from the past that still needs this prayer to be prayed?

Based on the truths you have just learned, what will you continue doing in your current relationships and what will you do differently?

What additional thoughts would you like to share with the others?

Chapter 2

Cover in Love

When people come into conflicts in relationships, they do not have to argue or quarrel to resolve them. One approach is to cover over the smaller issues in love.

In the section, "A Typical Scenario," the author describes an angry rant by a man over his step-daughter's actions which may require a reconciliation.

What is the scenario about?

What did the conflict concern?

What was the relationship between the parties?

Have you had a similar experience?

In the section, "A Scriptural Principle" the author presents an important biblical principle in the process of reconciliation which concerns covering over the smaller issues in love.

How would you express this principle in your own words?

How would you rewrite this principle to make it even more personal to your life (using your name and situation)?

Why do you think this principle might be important in your life right now?

How would you rate yourself on the percentage of times you followed this principle in the past when you did something wrong in a relationship?

Directions: Put a horizontal mark and your name where you see yourself on the percentage line.

0%   25%   50%   75%   100%

In the section, "A Biblical Explanation," the author explains the reasons why we should cover over the smaller issues in love and how to do it.

What is the first step in covering over the small things in love?

According to Proverbs 19:11, when someone sins against us what response brings honor to us?

What is the next step that should be taken if the issues are not as small?

What question can we ask ourselves to help us cover over a smaller sin or annoyance?

According to psalm 37:8, what action should we engage in to completely cover over an issue?

In what ways might these truths impact your relationships?

In the section, "An Ancient Portrait," the author provides an example of Abraham preventing a conflict with his nephew Lot by covering over an issue in love.

What conflict did Abraham anticipate might happen with Lot if he did not take action?

What choice did Abraham give to his nephew in order to avoid the conflict and cover over it in love?

What two reasons did Abraham probably have for covering over the potential conflict in love?

What were the consequences of Lot's selfish choice?

Though his nephew had taken the better land, how did his uncle show him he still loved him?

Have you ever been in a situation comparable to Abraham's prevention or Lot's choice? How was it different? How was it the same?

In the section, "A Modern Anecdote," the author discusses a situation where a husband and wife have become irritated over a variety of smaller issues in their relationship.

Who did the author ask the upset couple to focus on besides themselves and why?

What should we do with the strengths that the other person brings to our relationship?

What can we do with small annoyances or weaknesses of the other person that cannot be changed?

What should we do with the annoyances or weaknesses that can be or should be changed?

What should we do with the differences between us and the other person in the relationship?

Based on the truths learned in this chapter, what would you have done differently if you were the husband or wife?

In the section, "A Personal Response," the author provides a model you may use for prayer if you find it necessary after discovering the truths in this chapter.

Are you presently in a relationship where you have sinned against another and have not asked God for forgiveness? If not, is there one from the past that still needs this prayer to be prayed?

Based on the truths you have just learned, what will you continue doing in your current relationships and what will you do differently?

What additional thoughts would you like to share with the others?

Chapter 3

Resolve in Unity

Another way in which Christians can prevent arguments and quarreling is to proceed to a decision-making process. These are reserved for the more serious irritations, problems, and issues that arise.

In the section, "A Typical Scenario," the author describes an issue between a husband and wife that had not been settled, though the arguing had ended.

What is the scenario about?

What did the conflict concern?

What was the relationship between the parties?

Have you had a similar experience?

In the section, "A Scriptural Principle" the author presents an important biblical principle in the process of reconciliation which concerns a decision-making process for larger issues.

How would you express this principle in your own words?

How would you rewrite this principle to make it even more personal to your life (using your name and situation)?

Why do you think this principle might be important in your life right now?

How would you rate yourself on the percentage of times you followed this principle in the past when you did something wrong in a relationship?

Directions: Put a horizontal mark and your name where you see yourself on the percentage line.

| 0% | 25% | 50% | 75% | 100% |

In the section, "A Biblical Explanation," the author explains the reasons why we should deal with the larger issues in a decision making process and how to do it.

According to Romans 12:11 and 1 Corinthians 1:10, what should be the first two steps in the decision-making process and why?

According to 1 Thessalonians 5:21– 22, how do we actually make the decisions in the process?

According to 1 Corinthians 10:24 and 1 Peter 2:17, what is to be our motivation in the decision-making process?

According to Philippians 2:3–4, what should we be willing to do to find unity in the decision?

According to Proverbs 11:14 and 1 Corinthians 1:10, what should be done if a decision can't be made?

In what ways might these truths impact your relationships?

In the section, "An Ancient Portrait," the author provides an example of a conflict between Paul and Peter.

What was the conflict between Paul and the Judaizers?

How did Paul resolve the conflict with them?

What was the conflict Peter and Paul had?

How did Paul resolve it?

What was Peter's presumed response?

Have you ever been in any situation comparable to Paul's obligation to confront his fellow apostle or Peter's mistaken actions? How was it different? How was it the same?

In the section, "A Modern Anecdote," the author describes a conflict between two spouses over their parents.

Briefly, what did the conflict between the spouses concern?

What was the author's first step in resolving the issue?

What issues needed to be discussed in the decision-making process?

How did the couple resolve the issue?

How did the couple share it with their respective parents?

Based on the truths learned in this chapter, what would you have done differently if you were the husband or the wife with the different kind of parents?

In the section, "A Personal Response," the author provides a model you may use for prayer if you find it necessary after discovering the truths in this chapter.

Are you presently in a relationship where you have sinned against another and have not asked God for forgiveness? If not, is there one from the past that still needs this prayer to be prayed?

Based on the truths you have just learned, what will you continue doing in your current relationships and what will you do differently?

What additional thoughts would you like to share with the others?

Chapter 4

Utilize a Mediator

At times, believers will not be able to resolve a conflict or reconcile their relationship by themselves. When this occurs, they should seek a mediator.

In the section, "A Typical Scenario," the author describes a brother's issue with his sister that needed a mediator.

What is the scenario about?

What did the conflict concern?

What was the relationship between the parties?

Have you had a similar experience?

In the section, "A Scriptural Principle" the author presents an important biblical principle in the process of reconciliation which concerns the seeking of a mediator.

How would you express this principle in your own words?

How would you rewrite this principle to make it even more personal to your life (using your name and situation)?

Why do you think this principle might be important in your life right now?

How would you rate yourself on the percentage of times you followed this principle in the past when you did something wrong in a relationship?

Directions: Put a horizontal mark and your name where you see yourself on the percentage line.

0%   25%   50%   75%   100%

In the section, "A Biblical Explanation," the author explains the reasons why we should utilize a mediator if a conflict cannot be resolved and how to select one.

According to Galatians 6:1 and 1 Corinthians 6:5, what must we do if we are unable to reconcile with another?

What are some reasons why we may not be able to reconcile and need help?

What are the first four qualifications for choosing a mediator and why are they important?

What are the fifth and sixth qualifications that a mediator should possess and why are they important?

Where are three groups Christians can find mediators?

In what ways might these truths impact your relationships?

In the section, "An Ancient Portrait," the author provides an example of Paul mediating a reconciliation between a master and his runaway slave.

Why did Paul have to mediate a conflict between Onesimus and Philemon?

Why was Paul the perfect mediator for this issue?

What are some reasons Paul gave to Philemon to reconcile with Onesimus?

How did Paul want to handle the slave's possible theft?

How did Paul subtlety hold Philemon accountable for doing "the right thing"?

Have you ever been in a situation comparable to Philemon's betrayal, Onesimus' difficulty, or Paul's mediation? How was it different? How was it the same?

In the section, "A Modern Anecdote," the author describes a ministry conflict between an older and younger woman.

Why did the pastor put the two women together?

What different strengths did the two women bring to the relationship and ministry?

What weaknesses did each have which were manifested in their ministry?

What differences did the women bring to their relationship?

How did the two decide to utilize their strengths, support their weaknesses, and accept their differences?

Based on the truths learned in this chapter, what would you have done differently if you were the older, experienced woman or the younger, energetic woman?

In the section, "A Personal Response," the author provides a model you may use for prayer if you find it necessary after discovering the truths in this chapter.

Are you presently in a relationship where you have sinned against another and have not asked God for forgiveness? If not, is there one from the past that still needs this prayer to be prayed?

Based on the truths you have just learned, what will you continue doing in your current relationships and what will you do differently?

What additional thoughts would you like to share with the others?

Chapter 5

Refuse and Suffer

God does not want His children in conflict and strife with one another and with those outside the faith. So, when they refuse to reconcile, God steps in to discipline and train them.

In the section, "A Typical Scenario," the author describes an argument between a man and his father concerning the son's daughter which may require a reconciliation.

What is the scenario about?

What did the conflict concern?

What was the relationship between the parties?

Have you had a similar experience?

In the section, "A Scriptural Principle" the author presents an important biblical principle in the process of reconciliation which concerns Christians who refuse to reconcile.

How would you express this principle in your own words?

How would you rewrite this principle to make it even more personal to your life (using your name and situation)?

Why do you think this principle might be important in your life right now?

How would you rate yourself on the percentage of times you followed this principle in the past when you did something wrong in a relationship?

Directions: Put a horizontal mark and your name where you see yourself on the percentage line.

| 0% | 25% | 50% | 75% | 100% |

In the section, "A Biblical Explanation," the author explains the reasons why we must not refuse to reconcile with others and how God intervenes.

Why does God desire us to reconcile with others?

What is the first consequence if Christians refuse to reconcile the relationship?

In the discussion of the second and third consequences, why would the church or government become involved?

Concerning the fourth consequence, how might we suffer for our refusal inwardly?

According to the fifth consequence, what kind of heartache might others experience in the future if we refuse?

In what ways might these truths impact your relationships?

In the section, "An Ancient Portrait," the author describes the consequences that resulted when two half-brothers, sons of David, refused to reconcile.

What evil act did Amnon do that ruined his relationship with both his half-sister and her brother?

What did Absalom ask Tamar to do so he could take his own revenge?

How did Absalom treat Amnon after this evil?

What revenge did Absalom take on Amnon and how long had he planned it?

What should have Absalom done instead of taking revenge?

Have you ever been in a situation comparable to Amnon's evil, Absalom's revenge, or Tamar's horror? How was it the same? How was it different?

In the section, "A Modern Anecdote," the author describes a broken relationship between two friends who were pastors and how they reconciled.

What was the relationship like between the small and large church pastors?

How did the large church pastor create a deep rift between him and the other pastor?

What was the small church pastor's response?

What were some consequences of the small church pastor's refusal to reconcile with his pastor friend?

What did the small church pastor finally decide to do and what was the result?

Based on the truths learned in this chapter, what would you have done differently if you were small church pastor or the large church pastor?

In the section, "A Personal Response," the author provides a model you may use for prayer if you find it necessary after discovering the truths in this chapter.

Are you presently in a relationship where you have sinned against another and have not asked God for forgiveness? If not, is there one from the past that still needs this prayer to be prayed?

Based on the truths you have just learned, what will you continue doing in your current relationships and what will you do differently?

What additional thoughts would you like to share with the others?

Chapter 6

Love the Obstinate

No matter how hard we try, sometimes people remain upset or stubborn and will be unwilling to reconcile. When this happens God desires that we still show love to them.

In the section, "A Typical Scenario," the author describes a woman who refuses to attend an important family function which will require a reconciliation.

What is the scenario about?

What did the conflict concern?

What was the relationship between the parties?

Have you had a similar experience?

In the section, "A Scriptural Principle" the author presents an important biblical principle in the process of reconciliation which concerns the obstinance of others.

How would you express this principle in your own words?

How would you rewrite this principle to make it even more personal to your life (using your name and situation)?

Why do you think this principle might be important in your life right now?

How would you rate yourself on the percentage of times you followed this principle in the past when you did something wrong in a relationship?

Directions: Put a horizontal mark and your name where you see yourself on the percentage line.

0%	25%	50%	75%	100%

In the section, "A Biblical Explanation," the author explains the reasons why we should love the obstinate when they will not reconcile and how to do it.

According to Psalm 57:8, what does God think of retaliation?

According to 1 Thessalonians 5:15, what does the Lord God say we should do instead?

According to Philippians 1:9, how should we, as Christians, love, value, and prize those who oppose us?

What does it mean to bless those who oppose us?

Out of the different ways Jesus says that we should treat our enemies, which do you feel most comfortable with and why?

In what ways might these truths impact your relationships?

In the section, "An Ancient Portrait," the author describes the love of Jacob toward his uncle Laban when he sinned against Jacob and was obstinate in reconciling with him.

What was Laban's agreement with Jacob concerning Jacob's desire to marry Rachel?

How did Laban deceive Jacob on his wedding day and what was Jacob's righteous response?

How did Laban attempt to cheat Jacob out of the sheep he gave him and what was Jacob's righteous response?

Why did Jacob always respond righteously and not retaliate?

How did Laban desire to make peace with his nephew and what was Jacob's response?

Have you ever been in a situation comparable to Laban's treachery or Jacob's continual deception? How was it the same and how was it different?

In the section, "A Modern Anecdote," the author discusses a situation in which a close friendship developed between two women that quickly went sour and needed reconciliation.

How did Joyce establish a friendship with another worker?

What did Joyce's friend do that finally made her leave?

How did Joyce break up with her friend? Was it right?

What consequences did Joyce have to endure for breaking off her friendship without reconciling the relationship?

What did Joyce finally do to reconcile the relationship with her coworker?

Based on the truths learned in this chapter, what would you have done differently if you were Joyce who was annoyed by negativity or her friend who was abruptly dropped? How was it different? How was it the same?

In the section, "A Personal Response," the author provides a model you may use for prayer if you find it necessary after discovering the truths in this chapter.

Are you presently in a relationship where you have sinned against another and have not asked God for forgiveness? If not, is there one from the past that still needs this prayer to be prayed?

Based on the truths you have just learned, what will you continue doing in your current relationships and what will you do differently?

What additional thoughts would you like to share with the others?

Chapter 7

Battle and Rely

Since reconciliation is a divine process, it cannot be fully accomplished in our humanity alone. As a result, it might require time, a battle, and supernatural strength.

In the section, "A Typical Scenario," the author describes a brother's conflict with a sister that required a reconciliation.

What is the scenario about?

What did the conflict concern?

What was the relationship between the parties?

Have you had a similar experience?

In the section, "A Scriptural Principle" the author presents an important biblical principle in the process of reconciliation which concerns time, a battle, and supernatural strength.

How would you express this principle in your own words?

How would you rewrite this principle to make it even more personal to your life (using your name and situation)?

Why do you think this principle might be important in your life right now?

How would you rate yourself on the percentage of times you followed this principle in the past when you did something wrong in a relationship?

Directions: Put a horizontal mark and your name where you see yourself on the percentage line.

| 0% | 25% | 50% | 75% | 100% |

In the section, "A Biblical Explanation," the author explains the reasons why reconciliation may take time, a battle, and supernatural strength and how to acquire it.

What are the Lord God's two strength builders and how are they used?

What three enemies must we battle to restore a relationship?

What are two defensive pieces of armor that you think you need to make peace and reconcile?

What is the Sword of the Spirit and how do we utilize it in the reconciliation process?

What does the author call the spear and how do we utilize it in making peace in relationships?

In what ways might these truths impact your relationships?

In the section, "An Ancient Portrait," the author describes the relationship between Cain and Abel, the first two children of Adam and Eve.

What was the basic conflict between Cain and Abel?

What was Cain's response to the Lord's acceptance of Abel's offering?

What warning did God give Cain concerning sin?

What was Cain's solution to his conflict with Abel?

What was God's response to Cain as a result?

Have you ever been in any situation comparable to Abel's persecution for being righteous or Cain's jealousy? How was it different? How was it the same?

In the section, "A Modern Anecdote," the author discloses the conflict between two teachers over a red ball that needed reconciliation.

What was the older teacher's response to the kicking of the red ball?

What was the new teacher's response to this?

How did the conflict escalate on both sides?

How did the new teacher build the strength required to reconcile with the senior teacher?

Did the reconciliation occur all at once or take some time and why?

Based on the truths learned in this chapter, what would you have done differently if you were new teacher concerned about the kids or the senior teacher concerned about the rules?

In the section, "A Personal Response," the author provides a model you may use for prayer if you find it necessary after discovering the truths in this chapter.

Are you presently in a relationship where you have sinned against another and have not asked God for forgiveness? If not, is there one from the past that still needs this prayer to be prayed?

Based on the truths you have just learned, what will you continue doing in your current relationships and what will you do differently?

What additional thoughts would you like to share with the others?

Chapter 8

Act Like Him

To become motivated to utilize these reconciliation tools, Christians must focus on several goals that have to do with the character of God and acting like Him.

In the section, "A Typical Scenario," the author describes a woman who has decided to divorce her husband rather than reconcile with him.

What is the scenario about?

What did the conflict concern?

What was the relationship between the parties?

Have you had a similar experience?

In the section, "A Scriptural Principle" the author presents an important biblical principle in the process of reconciliation which concerns acting like God.

How would you express this principle in your own words?

How would you rewrite this principle to make it even more personal to your life (using your name and situation)?

Why do you think this principle might be important in your life right now?

How would you rate yourself on the percentage of times you followed this principle in the past when you did something wrong in a relationship?

Directions: Put a horizontal mark and your name where you see yourself on the percentage line.

| 0% | 25% | 50% | 75% | 100% |

In the section, "A Biblical Explanation," the author explains the reasons why we should act like God in order to desire reconciliation and how to do it.

Why should the knowledge of God's character motivate us to be more forgiving and seek reconciliation with others?

What are at least two reasons Christians should follow God's blueprint rather than man's?

What does it mean to be holy? How does it relate to seeking peace?

What is the difference between being a victim of man and a servant of God?

How did Jesus depend on this very truth at His arrest and crucifixion?

In what ways might these truths impact your relationships?

In the section, "An Ancient Portrait," the author shares how Jesus and Stephen were able to forgive and reconcile with their persecutors.

What were the different groups that Jesus asked the Father to forgive?

What would need to happen for them to be forgiven?

According to Luke 23:35–43, why does the thief suddenly receive forgiveness a few moments before his death?

What did the Jewish leaders do to Steven that instigated him to ask the Father for forgiveness?

Are forgiveness and desiring to reconcile natural responses?

Have you ever been in a situation comparable to Jesus or Stephen in which something terrible happened to you and you struggled with forgiveness and reconciliation? How was it different? How was it the same?

In the section, "A Modern Anecdote," the author explains the conflict that occurred between two physicians which would require reconciliation.

What was the past relationship the physicians had with each other?

How did the one physician respond to the other physician's success?

How did this express itself in words and behavior?

How did this effect the physician's relationship with God?

What changes in his divine perspective did the physician have to make to change his attitude?

Based on the truths learned in this chapter, what would you have done differently the less successful physician or the more successful physician?

In the section, "A Personal Response," the author provides a model you may use for prayer if you find it necessary after discovering the truths in this chapter.

Are you presently in a relationship where you have sinned against another and have not asked God for forgiveness? If not, is there one from the past that still needs this prayer to be prayed?

Based on the truths you have just learned, what will you continue doing in your current relationships and what will you do differently?

What additional thoughts would you like to share with the others?

Conclusion

As we conclude this book, I would like to leave us with some final thoughts about our God of reconciliation and what His Son did on the cross for us. First, if we understand the full extent of what was wrought for us on that cursed tree in order to make peace with us, it will become so much easier to do the same thing for others. Second, if you read this entire book and realized that you do not understand salvation or have never received Christ as Lord and Savior, then I would like to provide that opportunity. Please do not skip this section; it may be the most important in your life.

From all outward appearances, humans seem "good" and attempt to live decent lives. This is man's concept of himself. This is not God's concept. The Almighty's view is that people all over the world and throughout the ages sin, sin, and sin again (Romans 3:23). This is a terrible and utterly destructive condition. Yet, they have ramifications that are far worse. These sins condemn us to everlasting divine retribution.

Though described briefly in the Old Testament, the Lord Jesus Christ clearly announced and proclaimed the future punishment to come. Contrary to popular belief, Jesus did not only speak of love, grace, and mercy, He also spoke of the coming judgment for sin. He declared that the judgment of sin would be everlasting punishment in a place He called "Hell." The Lord portrayed this place as an eternal inferno (Matthew 18:8) where there would be the weeping (from the sorrow) and gnashing of teeth (from the agony and anguish of suffering) continually into eternity (Matthew 8:12; 13:42, 50; 22:13; 24:51; 25:30; Luke 13:28).

Why must people face this horrific punishment? Though God is a God of love, grace, and mercy, He is also a God of great holiness, righteousness, and justice (Psalm 89:14,18). These attributes are just as much a part of His divine nature as His love, grace, and mercy. You have broken God's law as we all have and the penalty must be paid. This began with the first man Adam (Genesis 3:1-7). When this occurred, His love, grace, and mercy surfaced and a provision was made. Someone else would have to take man's place and pay the penalty. Someone who had never transgressed Him, who would never deserve punishment, and would fulfill all of God's Laws, would be substituted in man's place. This was the Son of God, Jesus Christ.

As the God-Man, He would pay the penalty for our sins in His death on the cross. Once done, the Lord God made only one provision for people to appropriate what His Son had done on the cross for them. This provision is receiving Jesus Christ as Savior and Lord. Though I cannot possibly share with you this good news in the confines of this book, I would love for you to consider purchasing my book entitled, *Finding The Light: The Kingdom of Heaven and How To Enter It*. It can be found for sale on Amazon.com. It is inexpensive and contains the full gospel message for your consideration. This message is so important and extensive that it cannot adequately be contained in a few pages at the end of a book.

If you are a believer, you must go out into the world and seek peace through reconciliation as God did for us. These principles are to be lived and shared with others. You now have the tools to make your relationships last a lifetime. Go live them out and share them with others!

ABOUT THE AUTHOR

Dr. Donald Jones is currently a Christian Pastoral Counselor with thirty-eight years of experience in the fields of pastoral ministry, public education, and Christian counseling. He carries degrees and certificates from four major universities and from a variety of educational institutions. He has been a professor of Languages and Bible, a television commentator, and a featured speaker at a variety of events and seminars at churches, schools, and other organizations across the United States. He is a member in good standing of several secular and Christian professional organizations. Dr. Jones has been a published author since 1976. For further information view his website at www.donjonesphd.com.

www.ingramcontent.com/pod-product-compliance
Lightning Source LLC
Chambersburg PA
CBHW020041040426
42331CB00030B/451